HOW-TO LIBRARY

CREATING FAIRY RETREATS

By Dana Meachen Rau • Illustrated by Kathleen Petelinsek

CHERRY LAKE PUBLISHING • ANN ARBOR, MICHIGAN

CHERRY
LAKE
Publishing

Published in the United States of America by Cherry Lake Publishing
Ann Arbor, Michigan
www.cherrylakepublishing.com

Content Adviser: Dr. Julia L. Hovanec, Professor of Art Education,
Kutztown University, Kutztown, Pennsylvania

Photo Credits: Page 4, ©HTU/Shutterstock, Inc.; pages 5 and 6, ©Unholy
Vault Designs/Shutterstock, Inc.; pages 14 and 20, ©Dana Meachen Rau;
page 28, ©Michael Elliott/Dreamstime.com; page 29, ©Andrea Danti/
Shutterstock, Inc.; page 32, ©Tania McNaboe

Library of Congress Cataloging-in-Publication Data
Rau, Dana Meachen, 1971–
  Creating fairy retreats / by Dana Meachen Rau.
     pages cm — (Crafts) (How-to library)
  Includes bibliographical references and index.
  ISBN 978-1-61080-476-9 (lib. bdg.) —
ISBN 978-1-61080-563-6 (e-book) — ISBN 978-1-61080-650-3 (pbk.)
1. Handicraft. 2. Fairies. I. Title.
  TT157.R36 2012
  745.5—dc23   2012010573

Cherry Lake Publishing would like to acknowledge the work
of The Partnership for 21st Century Skills. Please visit
www.21stcenturyskills.org for more information.

Printed in the United States of America
Corporate Graphics Inc.
July 2012
CLFA11

TABLE OF CONTENTS

Fairies Among Us

Look for little lights in the early summer evening.

Have you seen blinking lights above the grass on a summer night? Maybe they are fireflies. Or maybe it's a troop of flying fairies. Did your room get cleaned while you were at school? Maybe it was your mom. Or perhaps a house fairy decided to lend a hand.

Many people like to imagine that fairies live among us. What do you think they would look like? It's fun to think that there is a world of fairies right outside your window or right inside your room. Stories tell of fairies that are helpful and some that are tricky. Fairies may do chores, help gardens grow, or dance in the grass. No matter what their job, fairies are busy!

Make your home, yard, or nearby park a welcome place for fairies. Create fairy **retreats** where they can take a break to rest and enjoy the treats you leave for them.

It's fun to imagine friendly creatures small enough to fit in an acorn.

Fairy Tales

People have made up many stories about fairies living among us.

For hundred of years, fairies have appeared in poems, plays, songs, and children's tales. Many of these stories began in Western Europe, in countries such as England, Ireland, and

Scotland. Many other cultures around the world also have stories of fairylike creatures.

The word *fairy* may refer to other types of magical creatures in **folklore**, too. Such creatures might include elves, giants, mermaids, witches, leprechauns, hobgoblins, or sprites. Fairies live on the land and in water. Some travel through the air. Many fairies keep to themselves. Others travel in groups.

Some storytellers imagined fairies as kind. Brownies were small men in brown, tattered clothes who came out at night and did chores to help families. The fairy godmother in the story "Cinderella" uses magic to help Cinderella get to the ball.

Other fairies caused trouble. Some kidnapped babies and brought them to fairyland. Pixies, little creatures dressed in green, **misled** travelers from their paths.

Some fairies in stories are the same size as humans. Others are tiny. Tinker Bell is a famous fairy created by author J. M. Barrie. She flies, sprinkles fairy dust, and has a voice that sounds like a tiny bell.

SHHHHH!
Fairies in stories are secretive. Some become invisible and only show themselves if they want Fairies hide the entrance to the world of fairyland.

Indoor Supplies

If you want to share your indoor space with fairies, you have to think small. What do you have around the house that's the right size for a tiny fairy? You can often reuse old containers and other items instead of throwing them away.

- *Empty plastic containers, cardboard boxes, baskets, ice cream sticks*—to build fairy furniture and retreats
- *Scraps of ribbon, buttons, plastic or silk flowers*—to decorate your fairy space
- *Old board game pieces, jacks, and marbles*—to entertain the fairies with tiny toys

Any materials that you use to make crafts can be used to make fairy items. Try to recycle old items when possible.

- *Cardboard, colored paper, glue, tape, scissors*—to create many different fairy retreats
- *Paint, markers, glitter*—to decorate your creations
- *Fabric, needle, thread, scissors*—to sew bedding, clothing, or other soft items for your fairies

You have the most important tool with you all the time. Your imagination! Imagine you are as tiny as a fairy. Crawl along the floor and explore small spaces. What supplies would be just the right size? Hunt for little items that you think your fairies will enjoy.

WHERE TO PLACE?
Place your fairy creations in corners, under beds, or in cabinets where shy fairies may feel hidden and safe.

9

Outdoor Supplies

Nature will provide you with most of the supplies you need for making outdoor fairies happy. Head out on a nature walk and bring along a basket or bag for collecting supplies.

- *Rocks, bark, hollow logs, and driftwood*—These larger items make good walls and spaces for fairy retreats.
- *Acorns, twigs, pinecones, seedpods, maple seeds, leaves, pine needles, vines*—These gifts from the trees can be made into extra items for your fairy retreat.
- *Dried grasses, flowers, pebbles, berries, burrs, antlers*—These gifts from the ground can be used to make fairy creations, too.
- *Shells, sand dollars, seaweed*—You can find these at the seashore.

- *Dried beans, avocado pits, onion skins, walnut shells, corn husks, eggshells*—You can find these scraps in the kitchen.

If you don't have an outdoor space to collect supplies, you can find some natural items at craft stores or garden shops. You can buy polished rocks, bags of shells, and other items to use for your fairy retreat.

WHERE TO BUILD

There are lots of out-of-the-way places to build a fairy home outdoors. Look for **sheltered** areas, such as hollow logs, cracks in rocks, or the crook of a tree. Find a soft flat area of moss or a tree stump. Look for hidden spaces under a bush or within the roots of a tree.

Fairies may also like to live in gardens. You can plant a real garden for your fairies in the ground or in a pot. You will need a trowel, soil and other gardening supplies. Have an adult help you choose the best place to plant your garden.

Fairy Furniture

Here are some tips for building and making items for your fairy retreats.

Sewing

Learn a simple running stitch:

1. Draw a light, straight line on the fabric. Thread your needle and knot the end.
2. Poke the needle up through the fabric. Pull it all the way through to the knot. Then poke it down into the fabric and pull it all the way through.
3. Repeat step 2 along your line until you reach the end. Try to keep your stitches even and straight. Tie a knot at the end.

Gluing

White glue works well for indoor crafts. It dries clear and cleans up easily. Use a glue gun to make outdoor items that will be **exposed** to rain or changing temperatures. Always ask an adult to help you with a hot glue gun.

Here's how to make a simple chair:

1. Find two small flat rocks or shells. Find four small pebbles or seeds.
2. Glue the pebbles/seeds on the underside of the "seat" rock/shell.
3. Glue the other rock/shell on the top of the seat as the back of the chair.

Tying

Here's how to tie sticks together with jute. Jute is a type of thin, strong rope:

1. Cross two twigs. Knot a small piece of jute diagonally across them.
2. Cross the strings under the back of the twigs. Then bring them around to the front and tie them diagonally the other way on top of your first knot. Trim off the extra.
3. Add more twigs onto these the same way. Place your creation up and down for a ladder or on its side for a fence.

Door in the Corner

Do fairies live in your house with you? Make a friendly fairy-size doorway to welcome fairies to their home sweet home.

Materials

Pencil and paper
Cardboard
Ruler
Scissors
Glue
Masking tape
Various colors of paint
    and markers
Paintbrushes
Brass fastener

Measure one inch from all the stoop's edges.

Steps

1. Decide what your door will look like. Sketch out your ideas with a pencil and paper.
2. First, make the front stoop. Cut a piece of cardboard to measure 6 x 7 inches (15 x 18 centimeters).

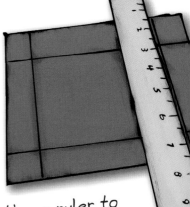

Use a ruler to measure and to make straight lines.

3. Measure and draw lines 1 inch (2.5) from each edge of the cardboard. **Score** the lines by lining up the ruler and running the pointy end of the scissors down each line.

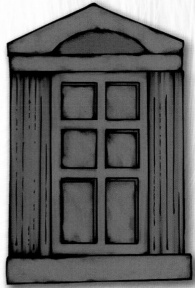

Bend the cardboard into a box shape.

4. Cut 1 inch into all four corners along the line to create four flaps.

5. Fold the cardboard along the scored lines to form a box shape. Tuck the square flaps into the corners. Glue them flat. Secure them on the inside of the box with masking tape.

6. To make the door, cut a piece of cardboard to measure 8 x 12 inches (20 x 30 cm).

7. Look at your sketch to see what details to add. Cut cardboard in a triangle for decoration above your door. Add thin rectangles of trim to look like wooden panels. You can use **corrugated** cardboard to make columns.

8. Glue all of these cardboard details onto the door piece of cardboard. Let the glue dry.

Add cardboard pieces to look like door details.

9. Paint the door, the trim, and the stoop a base color. It can be white, brown, or any color you want. You don't have to paint the back side of the stoop. It will be glued onto the door.

Paint a welcoming message on the door mat.

10. When the base color is dry, paint your door any color you want.

11. When the door paint is dry, have an adult help you poke a slit through one side of the door with the tip of your scissors. Place a brass fastener through the hole and secure it on the back. This will be the doorknob.

12. Paint your stoop to look like wood or stone. Add details with a marker.

13. When the stoop is dry, glue the back of the stoop to the base of the door. Let the glue dry.

14. Place the door in a corner of a room. When people spot it, they will be curious to know who lives in your walls!

Tooth Fairy Rest Stop

The tooth fairy has been busy all night collecting lost teeth. Make her a hammock so she can take a long nap after such a tiring evening.

Sew a soft spot for a fairy to sleep.

Materials

5 sheets of craft felt

Straight pins

Needle

Thread

Safety pin

2 long strips of tulle

Pencil

Scissors

Cotton balls or polyester stuffing

2 6-inch (15 cm) lengths of ribbon

1 small mug hook

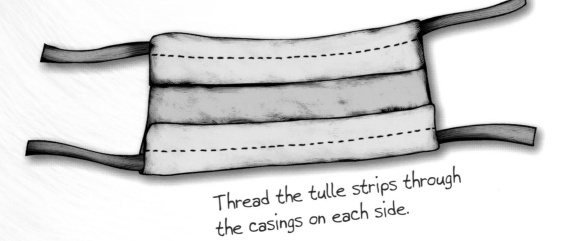

Fold and pin the long edges of a sheet of felt.

Steps

1. Fold both of
   the long sides
   of one sheet of felt
   about 2 inches (5 cm) in from the edge.
   Use straight pins to secure them in place.
2. Sew a running stitch up one of the sides,
   about ½ inch (1.3 cm) from the edge. Remove the pins.
   Repeat on the other side.
3. Stick a safety pin into the end of one of the strips of tulle.
   Be sure to close the pin so you don't poke your fingers.
   The safety pin will help you thread the tulle through the
   casing (tunnel) of felt on each side. Push it into one end
   of the casing. Carefully push it forward with one hand and
   pull it with the other, until it pokes out the other end. Pull
   the pin until you have an even length of tulle on each side
   of the casing. Repeat on the other side with the other strip
   of tulle.

Thread the tulle strips through the casings on each side.

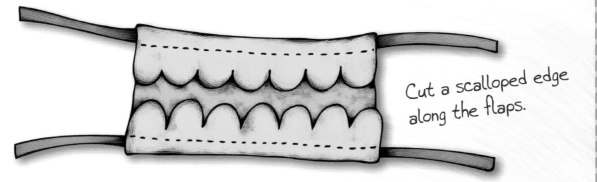

Cut a scalloped edge along the flaps.

4. Use a pencil to draw a **scalloped** edge on the two flaps. Use scissors to cut out the shapes.

5. Gently pull on both ends of the tulle to gather the felt in the center. This will make a cozy hammock shape.

6. Make flower decorations by cutting eight flower shapes and four leaf shapes out of felt. Stack them with one leaf shape on the bottom and two flower shapes on top.

7. Sew the shapes together by poking a needle from the bottom of the stack to the top and back down again. Then sew the flower onto one corner of your hammock. Repeat on the other three corners.

8. Make a pillow by cutting a piece of felt to measure 6 x 6 inches (15 x 15 cm). Place some cotton balls or stuffing in the middle close to one edge of the felt.

9. Roll the felt from one end to the other to form a tube shape. Secure it with a straight pin. Tie ribbon in a tight bow on each end. Remove the pin.

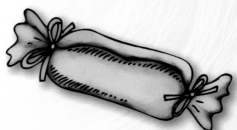

10. Have an adult help you secure the mug hook in the ceiling. Tie the tulle ends in a bow and hang your hammock.

Wishing Web

Hang wishing webs on a tree to catch fairy wishes. Natural items, such as grapevines, feathers, and pinecones, make perfect building materials and decorations.

Materials

About 3 or 4 lengths of
grapevine, about 1 yard
(1 meter) each
Jute
Scissors
Feathers, pinecones, or other
natural decorations

Hang a web to catch wishes!

Steps

1. Bend a length of grapevine in a loop and tie the ends together with a small piece of jute. Weave the edges of the grapevine around the loop and tie them to form a circle shape.
2. Tie the center of another branch to the top of the loop. Weave it around the circle and tie the ends. Continue adding branches to make a wreath of vines.

3. Cut a length of jute about 2 yards (1.8 m) long. Tie one end to the top of the wreath. Wind the rest into a ball so it will be easier to handle.

4. Loop the jute around the edge of the wreath by weaving it behind the back, over the front, and through the loop. Pull tight.

5. Continue making loops around the wreath until you reach the top again.

6. Continue a second round of loops. This time, make loops on the jute in between the loops of the previous round.

7. Continue looping around and around until you reach the center of the wreath.

Loop the jute around and around until you reach the center.

8. Tie the jute onto the center of the web with a knot and trim off the extra jute.

9. Tie a loop of jute on the top of your web for hanging.

10. Cut three lengths of jute to measure about 12 inches (30 cm) long. Tie them along the bottom of the wreath. Attach feathers, pinecones, or other natural decorations to the hanging ends.

Cabin in the Tiny Woods

To a fairy, a pot of plants seems like a forest. Grow plants, add natural details, and make homemade decorations to create a cabin in the woods for a fairy.

Materials

1 large clay pot
Pencil and paper
Trowel
1 bag potting soil
2 or 3 easy-to-grow
    houseplants
Watering can
Twigs
Glue gun
Small milk carton
Spanish moss
3 or 4 pinecones
Grass seed
6 to 8 small flat rocks
Mist spray bottle

A pot of plants looks
like a forest to a fairy.

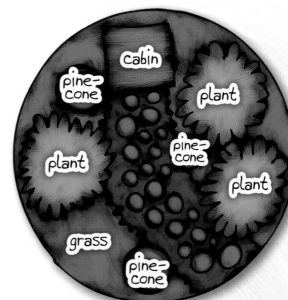

Steps

1. Trace the top of the pot onto a piece of paper. Use this circle to draw a **blueprint** of your fairy pot. Decide where you want to place your cabin, plants, and pathway.

2. Use the trowel to fill your pot with potting soil about an inch (2.5 cm) from the top. You might want to do this outside or on a surface spread with newspapers to keep things clean.

3. Dig holes into the surface of the soil. Place the plants in these holes. Pack the soil around them and water them well.

4. Make your fairy cabin. Break twigs into 2- to 3-inch (5 to 8 cm) lengths. Have an adult help you use a glue gun to stick the twigs onto the sides of the milk carton. Glue Spanish moss onto the top of the carton to cover the roof.

5. Place your cabin in the pot. Add pinecones to look like evergreen trees.

6. Sprinkle grass seed onto the open areas. Gently press the seeds into the soil. Then place a path of rocks onto the grass.

7. Place the pot in a sunny or shady spot in your home, depending on the types of plants and grass seed you used. Every day or so, spray the seeds with a mist spray bottle to keep them moist so they will grow. Water your plants about every week, or more often if they seem dry.

Fairy Feast

Dinnertime for fairies is best enjoyed outdoors.

Set an inviting table for fairies to enjoy a meal with their fairy friends.

Materials

Tree stump

4 to 6 rocks

Acorn caps

Small pinecones

Twigs

Dried gourd or walnut shell

Berries, leaves, seeds, or other natural items

Steps

1. Find a flat tree stump to use as a table. Surround it with rocks to look like chairs.
2. Place the acorn caps on the table to look like plates. Place the pinecones to look like cups.
3. Find twigs that branch out in a fork shape. Find others that are straight like knives. Place one of each at each plate.
4. Place the bottom of the gourd in the center of the table. Fill this bowl with a variety of natural items. You can add berries, autumn leaves, white wisps from milkweed pods, maple seeds, or any other colorful natural items that look like they might be tasty for fairies.

RESPECTING NATURE

Try not to disturb nature while you are collecting your materials. Don't pick live plants or flowers. Check the ground and only collect discarded or fallen items. In your own yard, some plants may need to be trimmed to stay healthy. You may be able to use some of the branches or flowers that an adult cuts off for you.

Rock Wall Hotel

Create a fun space
for a fairy getaway.

Fairies need a place to take a vacation. Build them a hotel
next to a stone wall, complete with a swimming hole and a
playground for them to take a break from all of their chores.

Materials

A stone wall

Trowel

Plastic container

Sand

A bunch of medium-size
flat rocks

Smaller flat rocks and
tiny pebbles

Glue gun

Twigs

Jute

Bark

Branch with offshoots

Steps

The pool area

1. In front of the wall, dig a small hole just big enough to hold your plastic container. Set the container into the hole so the top of the container is level with the ground.
2. Sprinkle some sand around the pool.
3. Stack three flat rocks on the edge of the pool to make a diving board.
4. Make two pool chairs out of the small flat rocks and pebbles with the glue gun (*see page 13*).
5. Make a ladder from the twigs and jute (*see page 13*). Place it on the edge of the diving board.

Poolside chairs give fairies a place to sit.

The pool house

1. Stack several flat rocks into two or three columns.
2. Place two pieces of bark on top to form the roof.

The playground
1. Stick the branch into the ground.
2. Tie jute onto one large twig to make a swing.
   Tie them to one of the branch offshoots.
3. Make fairy fences out of twigs and jute (*see page 13*). Place it around the playground area.

The hotel
1. Make a bunch of fairy ladders (*see page 13*).
2. Place some of the ladders along the ground at the base of the wall. Place others among the rocks of the wall. It will look like the ladders lead to the spaces in between the rocks, where you can imagine fairies are hiding and relaxing in their hotel rooms.

MORE THAN FAIRIES
Fairies aren't the only creatures who will visit your hotel. Birds especially may enjoy a drink or splash in the pool.

New Point of View

Find a friend and search for fairies together.

When you look at the world as a fairy does, you get a new view. Indoors, you may notice more details and spaces than you ever did before. You may even notice how dusty the corners can be! Outdoors, you may notice new colors, shapes, and gifts that nature gives us to enjoy.

Invite over some friends on a rainy day to make fairy retreats. Spend a sunny day outside exploring and building. Use your imagination. It's fun to think that secret helpful fairy friends are watching out for you. Watch out for them by making treats and retreats to show them how special they are.

Glossary

blueprint (BLOO-print) a plan for building something

casing (KAY-sing) a tunnel of fabric

corrugated (KOR-uh-gay-tid) having ridges

discarded (dis-KAHR-did) thrown away or set aside

exposed (ik-SPOSED) open or unprotected

folklore (FOHK-lor) the stories told by a particular culture

misled (mis-LED) tricked

retreats (ri-TREETS) quiet places for resting

scalloped (SKAL-uhpd) having a bumpy edge like a scallop shell

score (SKOHR) to make an indented line in paper

sheltered (SHEL-turd) protected

More Ideas

Use these further ideas as sparks to make unique fairy retreats of your own!

INDOORS

- Use a bowl for a bathtub, a washcloth as a towel and a sliver of soap for a fairy bath.
- Set up a fairy picnic with a cloth napkin blanket, checker piece plates, and toothpaste cap cups.
- Stack cans and boxes in the cupboard to make a fairy apartment house.

OUTDOORS

- Make a pumpkin castle with carved doors and windows and dried ears of corn as turrets.
- Create a beach retreat with driftwood, a shell bed, and a seaweed blanket.
- Build boats of bark for fairies to ride down a stream.

For More Information

Books

Barker, Cicely Mary. *Fairyopolis: A Flower Fairies Journal.* London: Penguin Books, 2005.

Burns, Jan. *Fairies.* Detroit: KidHaven Press, 2007.

Monaghan, Kimberly. *Organic Crafts: 75 Earth-Friendly Art Activities.* Chicago: Chicago Review Press, 2007.

Niehaus, Alisha. *Fairypedia.* New York: DK Publishing, 2009.

Web Sites

Disney Family Fun: Nature Crafts

http://familyfun.go.com/crafts/home-garden-projects/gardening-nature-crafts/nature-crafts/

Enjoy other fun craft projects using natural materials.

Do It Yourself: Make Dollhouse Furniture out of Everyday Items

www.doityourself.com/stry/make-dollhouse-furniture-out-of-everyday-items#b

Learn how to make all kinds of furniture to decorate your fairy retreats.

Index

About the Author

Dana Meachen Rau is the author of more than
300 books for children on many topics, including
science, history, cooking, and crafts. She creates,
experiments, researches, and writes from her home
office in Burlington, Connecticut.